Praise for *Fiqh of Social Media*

"With the time we spend on social media, being mindful of how we use it is crucial. This is a wonderful resource based in prophetic guidance on how to practically use social media in wise and beneficial ways."

-Dr. Omar Suleiman, Yaqeen Institute

"Reading Fiqh of Social Media is like sitting with your best friend from Sunday school and having an intellectual & spiritual conversation about the impact of social media on your life. Omar distills years of research, experience, and thought leadership in an easily digestible book that you can enjoy with a good cup of coffee (and your phone off!)"

-Mohammed Faris, The Productive Muslim Company

"Having followed Omar Usman's extensive work on the #FiqhOfSocialMedia and attended the seminar by him in person, I'm thrilled to hear about this being released in book form. Behavioral experts often demarcate an addiction by its rendering of a person dysfunctional; it sabotages his/her career, relationships, health, or any other fundamental facet of one's life. Therefore, considering what the digital age is undeniably crippling in our lives, I cannot overstate the importance of availing oneself this sobering critique of social media's true costs, its pragmatic course for rehabilitation, and its showcasing of the renewed relevance of Islam's timeless principles for self-care in the most comprehensive sense of the word."

-Shaykh Mohammad Elshinawy, Mishkah University

"In a time when social media is such a huge part of our lives, Br. Omar's work is an important read. He shares insightful reflections and sound advice, drawing from Islamic teachings and wisdom in an approachable and easy to understand way. This is an excellent guidebook, offering practical strategies to make our social media usage spiritually healthy, balanced and beneficial."

-SHAYKHA SHAZIA AHMAD

"From the nostalgia of growing as a teen in the 90's to the challenges that parents face in this day and age the Fiqh of Social Media by Omar Usman is an easy read that offers practical advice on how to navigate the social media world through an Islamic lens. Emphasizing the most important points, in a concise fashion, it serves as a great guide for teens and parents for protecting themselves and navigating through all of the challenges that come with the online world. If I was to summarize it in three words: Practical Spirituality Online. Highly recommended for all."

-SHAYKH NAVAID AZIZ, ALMAGHRIB INSTITUTE

"The Prophet ﷺ said, "Whoever believes in Allah and the Last Day should say something good or keep silent." The ability to control our tongues, how we communicate with others, is an expression of our faith. Communication has evolved and changed so much that one of the primary ways many of us communicate with others is through social media; hashtags and 280 characters. This is a long-awaited work from my good friend and Hajj companion Omar Usman who has been writing, tweeting, speaking, and teaching about the Fiqh of Social Media for years. This is a valuable work providing guidance on how to use and benefit from social media in a way that conforms to our principles and values."

-SHAYKH FURHAN ZUBAIRI, INSTITUTE OF KNOWLEDGE

"Ulama of the past have written on the Adaab of speech and social interaction. Connecting those guidelines with the modern world of social media has been the need of our time. May Allah reward Omar for taking this task on!"

-MUFTI HUSSAIN KAMANI, QALAM INSTITUTE

"Alhamdulillah, I'm so thankful for this much-needed work by Omar Usman. As we continue to live more and more online, it is imperative that we reflect deeply on the opportunities that social media presents as well as the unique, and often dangerous, challenges. May Allah accept from Omar and may this book inspire these important conversations to be had in our families and communities."

-SHAYKH AMMAR ALSHUKRY, ALMAGHRIB INSTITUTE

"Social media and technology have become a major part of our lives. Not only that, they are changing the way we live in very significant ways, making this an extremely important topic for every Muslim to understand. This concise, to-the-point book provides practical advice on how to deal with social media in light of Islamic teachings. It demonstrates that the guidance of Islam is not only timeless, but as timely as ever."

-SHAYKH SALMAN NASIR, LEGACY INSTITUTE

"Omar Usman's Fiqh of Social Media is a useful explanation of a major overarching Islamic jurisprudence principle that states:

'Giving a ruling on a matter is a function of understanding its reality.' The book renders an essential service of helping American Muslims understand the intricacies of social media in-depth, from its sources to its solutions. How we approach the plethora of informational outlets around us and steer through what's best for our Deen is critical in achieving a balance. Omar's nuanced discussion is helpful in formulating an Islamic framework for addressing this topic."

-SHAYKH NOMAAN BAIG, INSTITUTE OF KNOWLEDGE

"A welcome contribution that weaves together a wide array of resources to help Muslims navigate the rough terrain of social media."

-MUFTI MUNTASIR ZAMAN, QALAM INSTITUTE

"The Prophet ﷺ says, 'The best of people are those who are most beneficial to people.' This work serves as a practical guide for a tool that dominates so much of our personal, professional, and spiritual lives. We likely spend more time on social media than we do on several other important aspects of our lives. An Islamic framework to guide our interactions with it is long overdue. Omar explores this important topic through the guidance of the Qur'an and Sunnah while coupling it with basic action items that you can immediately implement. It should be required reading for both children and adults, and ultimately worked into Islamic School curriculums. I have personally attended a portion of the Fiqh of Social Media seminar and am excited to see this book come to fruition. Taking the time to read and implementing the action items will improve your life, your relationship with Allah, your family and 'friends.' I ask Allah to reward Omar for his efforts and put this in his scale of good deeds."

-Shaykh Mohamed Hussein, Graduate Islamic University of Madinah - College of Hadith

"I found Fiqh of Social Media relevant to me as a mother, a wife and someone whose advocacy work demands copious usage of social media. Omar Usman doesn't dictate or lull you with listicles but forces you to think deeply about you and your family's situation and usage of social media, using Prophetic reminders. A culmination of lessons from his online writings and workshop with the same moniker, this book will help save the reader from making avoidable social and spiritual faux pas."

-Hena Zuberi, Editor in Chief, Muslimmatters

"This is a must-read for Muslims around the globe. I can't thank Omar enough for this work which forces Muslims to look in the mirror and answer tough questions about how social media has impacted our lives. It questions why we desire to share the most intimate aspects of our lives with strangers from around the world and provides action items to implement. These discussions need to be had within the Muslim community. We have to question how our quality of life has been impacted by the age of hyper-connectivity. Due to the fact that Social Media is the tool for creating social capital, we need to realize that speaking about the harms of constant connectivity takes a lot of courage. Thank you, Omar, for this work."

-Shaykh Mikaeel Smith, Qalam Institute

© 2021 Omar Usman. All rights reserved.

No part of this publication may be reproduced, stored in a retrieval system, or transmitted in any form or by any means, electronic or otherwise, including photocopying, recording, and internet without prior permission of Omar Usman.

Title: *Fiqh of Social Media*
ISBN: 979-8575659563
First Edition

Author:	Omar Usman
Proofreader:	Zainah Usman
Cover Design:	Amnah Sultan

//
FIQH OF SOCIAL MEDIA

Timeless Islamic Principles for Navigating the Digital Age

OMAR USMAN

For my family.
After the blessings of Allah,
without their support,
none of this would be possible.

Contents

	Foreword	XIII
	Introduction	XV
CHAPTER 1	#Intention	1
CHAPTER 2	#Friendship	3
CHAPTER 3	#Phone	12
CHAPTER 4	#Reflect	16
CHAPTER 5	#Takathur	21
CHAPTER 6	#PublicizingSins	24
CHAPTER 7	#Family	30
CHAPTER 8	#Envy	37
CHAPTER 9	#Change	43
CHAPTER 10	#EchoChambers	52
CHAPTER 11	#Nasihah	58
CHAPTER 12	#2Faces	70
CHAPTER 13	#Spirituality	74
CHAPTER 14	#Optimism	81
CHAPTER 15	#ActionPlan	86
	Conclusion	93
	Acknowledgements	94
	Also by the Author	96

Foreword

The logicians defined the human being in Arabic as *al-ḥay-awān al-nāṭiq*, which translates to "animal endowed with speech" or "rational living being." The faculty to formulate meaning, achieve clarity, and intelligently express thoughts is what distinguishes the human being from other living creatures.

Allah says in the Qur'an, "It is God who brought you out of your mothers' wombs knowing nothing, and gave you hearing and sight and minds, so that you might be thankful."[1] We are informed in the Qur'an that our ability to communicate ideas and understanding is one of the greatest gifts and blessings bestowed upon us, "It is the Lord of Mercy - who taught the Qur'an. - He created man - and taught him to communicate."[2] As with all abilities, it comes with responsibility. Allah states in the Qur'an, "speak good words to all people."[3] He condemns the liars, forbids slander and backbiting, and commands us to keep our promises. In summary, Islam instructs and guides us in every aspect of our lives, including communication. Social media and online interactions are not an exception.

---

1 16:78
2 55:1-4
3 2:83

We often hear that social media isn't real life, but it is a reflection of it. It can feel artificial and distant, like staring into a mirage, but it affects our lives in a very real way. I must admit that I am not very keen on social media. I am skeptical of its purported benefits. This is largely due to the major benefits of social media being economic and business related, while the harms are primarily spiritual, emotional, psychological, and social. However, I cannot deny that it is embedded in people's lives and cultures, and therefore extremely difficult to avoid. We are in need of detailed discussions regarding its usage and function. The effects of social media on our hearts, families, communities, and societies has to be evaluated and managed.

I am grateful and appreciative of my friend, Omar Usman, for exhausting available resources; Islamic, psychological, secular, and business, to develop the work you see before you. We have had long discussions pertaining to many of the topics covered in this book. I am confident that you will find this book to be beneficial, and I pray that it inspires more contributions on this topic.

The timeless principles and wisdom of our religion have navigated us through the challenges of the past and will continue to do so in the future.

-ABDULNASIR JANGDA
QALAM INSTITUTE

Introduction

It started when I asked my father to buy me the new gaming system all the other kids were getting - a Nintendo. I had played Duck Hunt at a friend's house, and could not wait to get my own. Fearful of fostering a crippling video game addiction (way ahead of his time on that one), he opted for the more "educational" option and bought a home computer instead.

Since then, I've always been in the computer field one way or another. I learned how to make webpages by teaching myself HTML in middle school. In college, I majored in Computer Science, and have since gone on to spend my professional career in the IT industry.

Along the way, alhamdulillah, I was fortunate to be a founding member of Qalam Institute, MuslimMatters, and worked with a number of other local and national Islamic organizations. Working with these organizations exposed me to the true impact of these social technologies. I learned what it took to build an online community from scratch, and how to leverage social media to get beneficial content in front of as many people as possible. This was different from the type of volunteering I grew up with like teaching at Sunday school or setting up *iftar* at the local masjid during Ramadan.

Alongside these societal changes was a much more disruptive one - the change to our personal lives. Within the span of a few years, we have gone from most college students not having laptops, to seeing 2-year-olds finding videos to watch on a phone or tablet.

These changes have been so rapid that we have not had a chance to pause and collect our thoughts. We have not properly grappled with how to use them in a way that lets us utilize their benefits while also avoiding their harmful consequences.

The Fiqh of Social Media was born out of this need to assess our interaction with these new technologies. In particular, there seemed to be a disconnect in understanding basic Islamic principles and applying them to online interactions.

The project started with a small publication of *The 40 Hadith on Social Media*, and from there, alhamdulillah, turned into a traveling family night program through Qalam Institute taught in communities all across the US for the past 5 years.

Throughout those travels, I have had the opportunity to discuss these topics in detail with all different types of people. They have shared the impact of social media on themselves, their families, and their communities.

This book is a culmination of those experiences and conversations.

CHAPTER ONE

#INTENTION

The Prophet ﷺ said, "Actions are by intentions, and every person will be rewarded according to what he has intended."[4]

The year 1985 is a dividing line for understanding how people think about technology[5]. Those born before that year are the last generation of mankind to meaningfully experience adult life without smartphones or social media. Those born after are considered "digital natives" who see everything around them simply as the way things have always been.

If you were born before 1985, you probably remember taking notebooks to class instead of laptops, stopping at a gas station to ask directions instead of using GPS, and answering a phone call without knowing who was on the other end.

We may feel nostalgia for the good old days before the internet, but we cannot reverse technological progress no matter how much we want to. It is easy to see images from tech conferences with a thousand audience members all wearing VR headsets and get scared about the future.

---

4   Bukhārī and Muslim
5   Michael Harris, *End of Absence*

Technology itself will continue to evolve and change. Islam is timeless. Basic human needs and human psychology remain the same.

Simon Mainwaring, a thought leader in the space of social media, aptly summarized the role of technology, "Like all technology, social media is neutral but is best put to work in the service of building a better world."

It is therefore imperative that we learn how social media and similar technologies impact our lives and address the manner in which we interact with them. The focus of this book is understanding the framework Islam gives us for managing our relationship with technology and social media – and therefore not about specific platforms that come and go. Our faith teaches us how to lead in times of change, enabling us to utilize technology positively for ourselves, our families, and our communities.

The intention is to stay focused on the bigger picture principles that will equip a person with the correct mindset and approach, no matter how much actual technologies and platforms change.

This book is written with the goal of covering some of the broader themes associated with social media usage. The chapters are structured to provide a reflection followed by action items for you to complete.

It is my hope, *insha'Allah*, that this provides a starting point for people to build on, and fosters discussions in your local Islamic centers, friends circles, and book clubs.

CHAPTER TWO

#FRIENDSHIP

When my son wants to play videogames with his friends, he sends out a group text, turns on the game, and puts on a gaming headset, ready to go.

When I wanted to play videogames with my friends, it was a completely different process. First, I'd have to tell my parents which friend I wanted to play with. If they weren't a pre-approved friend, then there was an interview process. Who is this person? What kind of grades does he make? What do his parents do for a living? How many siblings does he have?

If my friend passed this tough job interview, then he was allowed to come over to my house with his Nintendo (since I didn't have one) and an extra controller so we could play Mario-Kart.

Communicating with friends was another challenge. We had the dreaded "house phone" that everyone had to share. Calling a friend meant having to first make small talk with one of his parents before they handed over the phone.

Eventually, we made the move to AIM: AOL Instant Messenger (Rest in Peace) where we could chat unencumbered by the limitations of the house phone. AIM, in hindsight, was only a domino in what would eventually become the social media revolution. I still maintain that the AIM Away Message is the original Twitter.

ICQ, MSN, and other chat tools grew in popularity and created mini-online communities. Old school bulletin board systems (BBSs) now became gigantic message board platforms where you could find like-minded people, make new virtual friends, and debate with others. Facebook exploded across college campuses. Internet debates we see now in comments sections and private group texts existed exactly the same way in BBSs and private email lists.

Social media was not only a communication revolution, it was a friendship and relationship revolution. Never before in human history have people been able to make friendships at such a large scale without any prior relationship.

The speed and pace of friendships has changed drastically. In a traditional friendship, you are exposed to personal details over time. In the digital age, what used to take months to learn about someone is now instant. You meet people at an event, add them on social media, and suddenly you know their whole life. You can see every place they've vacationed, what each of their family members looks like, their favorite sports team, which restaurants they frequent, what the inside of their home looks like, political affiliations, and mutual acquaintances.

One-way friendships are uniquely enabled by social media. We follow people we want to connect with even if they don't follow us back. This goes far beyond following celebrities or athletes. You may follow the account of someone in your city that frequents new restaurants, and in doing so become exposed to multiple facets of that person's life – even though they have no idea you even exist.

These new dynamics of friendships and relationships mean we need better foundational principles to govern these interactions.

The Prophet ﷺ said, "The similitude of good company and that of bad company is that of the musk (perfume) seller and of the blacksmith. The musk seller would either offer you some free of charge, or you would buy it from him, or you smell its pleasant fragrance. As for the blacksmith, he either burns your clothes, or you smell something repugnant."[6]

Who we follow *is* the company we keep. It's all the accounts we follow and the people in our group chats. We receive hundreds of messages from them all throughout the day.

Consider the example of a casual acquaintance that you follow online. You rarely meet this person or even exchange messages with them, but you see them posting a dozen times a day about how much they dislike their family or how annoying their parents are. What is the subconscious effect of seeing these messages daily?

Or consider the example of a celebrity you admire and follow. They may post some useful and interesting content, or even promote products you're interested in purchasing. But what is the effect when you regularly see pictures they post that may be inappropriate?

---

6 Bukhārī and Muslim

We overestimate our ability to filter the good from the bad. Constant exposure is not healthy.

Taking this hadith a step further, we find the Prophet ﷺ saying, "A man is upon the religion of his friend, so let one of you look at whom he befriends."[7]

This hadith is a profound insight into the human mind. It shows that who we associate with affects our subconscious much more than we'd like to admit. It also shows that a good friendship means knowing one another on a deep level. True friendship means being comfortable with their value system, beliefs, ethics, and character.

One pitfall of social networking is the idea of hyper-connectivity. The abundance of superfluous connections sometimes gives the false impression of meaningful interactions. Brady Quinn, who was the quarterback of the Kansas City Chiefs football team when one of their teammates committed suicide, made this statement:

> "The one thing people can hopefully try to take away, I guess, is the relationships they have with people," Quinn told reporters after the game. "I know when it happened, I was sitting and, in my head, thinking what I could have done differently. When you ask someone how they are doing, do you really mean it? When you answer someone back how you are doing, are you really telling the truth?
>
> We live in a society of social networks, with Twitter pag-

---

7 Tirmīdhī

> es and Facebook, and that's fine, but we have contact with our work associates, our family, our friends, and it seems like half the time we are more preoccupied with our phone and other things going on instead of the actual relationships that we have right in front of us. Hopefully, people can learn from this and try to actually help if someone is battling something deeper on the inside than what they are revealing on a day-to-day basis."[8]

Your closest friends are usually people you have known for a long time. Strong friendships go through ups and downs. If you encounter an argument or some type of conflict, you find a way to work through it and come out stronger on the other end. What happens now is that when a friendship is tested, there is no longer an incentive to make an investment into that relationship. Instead, people can see that they are connected to hundreds of other friends (or potential friends) through social networks. The old friend is easily replaceable by someone else.

It does not take a huge leap of logic to see then why platforms such as Facebook are listed more and more commonly as causes of divorce. People thrive on this feeling of connectivity. They start to connect with exes who they otherwise would not have talked to. If they get frustrated with their spouse, they can easily find someone else to talk to and connect with instead of fixing their relationship.

---

8 NBC Sports (https://profootballtalk.nbcsports.com/2012/12/03/brady-quinns-poignant-comments-on-relationship/)

There is an unprecedented level of speed and accessibility in creating relationships and connections with others. Bonds are rapidly established due to the ease with which you identify common interests. When you find someone quickly, and they share common interests, and they give you attention – trust also develops quickly. Needless to say, this is not always a healthy type of trust.

The manner in which we confide personal details to others online requires a high level of caution. When going through the ups and downs of a friendship, relationship, job issue, or family issue, it is natural to seek advice from others or even vent to others.

We can find valuable guidance for the digital age in these words of Alī, "Love the one whom you love moderately, perhaps one day he will be someone for whom you have hatred, and hate the one whom you hate moderately, perhaps one day he will be one whom you love."[9]

Umar also states, "Do not let your love be an obsession, nor your hate destruction." He was asked, "How so?" He responded, "When you love, you are clingy like a child, and when you hate, you wish destruction for your companion."[10]

The obvious implication is to not over-share as you may later regret it. Everything on the internet is forever. Private conversations can be screenshotted and leaked at any time.

This should be a point of education for families as well. Par-

---

9   Bukhārī, *Adab al-Mufrad*
10 Bukhārī, *Adab al-Mufrad*

ents should teach children what is appropriate to share online and what is not. We need a renewed sense of awareness regarding what personal details are for public consumption and what is not – regardless of the supposed privacy settings of the apps you are using.

Not everyone who is "your friend" is actually your friend or has your best interests at heart. Not everyone "following" you online is actually a fan. Imam Tahir Anwar explains this well in a post to his Facebook page:

> "Just because some people post pictures of themselves, their children or their lives on Facebook, others think they are very happy. And happy they may be, but that doesn't mean their lives are perfect. A few comments or check-in's doesn't mean they don't have worries in life. So when you see them, don't become jealous.
>
> Too many people are complaining of going through calamity after calamity, and the "evil eye" or "nazar" could be a possible reason.
>
> Not everyone is your friend. Even your closest friends may not be your friends. Only time and calamities in your life will prove who is your friend. Most people are merely acquaintances. If you don't believe what I have to say, just ask yourself. How many of the people you hang out with, do you backbite? (Speaking the truth behind their backs is backbiting, otherwise it's slander!)
>
> Be careful as to what you share on Facebook. With the new privacy settings, there IS not privacy. As an Imam, I

> know of many people who have admitted to stalking other people's profiles and pictures, and doing unmentionable things in private.
>
> And there are many who are jealous of you, based on the few good things they know about you. Be conscious about what you share.
>
> This lesson is for me first, then others."

Social media is an envy amplifier. It is easy to look at someone's timeline and assume that everything is perfect for them. They are sharing photos of their perfect family, fancy foods, and exotic vacation. Meanwhile, it feels like you are sitting there with all these problems and struggles that no one else is dealing with. This is a recipe for developing *ḥasad* (envy). The same is true the other way around as well. Be careful of what you share because you may incite *ḥasad* in others.

This is one way that a person who loves you, may one day develop hatred for you.

Disliking someone in moderation is easier to put into context for the digital age. The easy rule of thumb is to simply stay silent when you do not like someone.

One of the most destructive practices online is trolling and bullying. This type of behavior is contagious and encourages people to pile on and join in (sometimes anonymously). We should resist that behavior even with those we dislike.

Friendships shape us in more ways than we realize. We can no longer differentiate online and offline personas. Both have a tangible impact, and we need to be cognizant of the Islamic principles and how to live by them no matter how much the systems and environment around us change.

Following a brand or a general account is another type of online persona even though it may not be linked to a specific person. Take media accounts as an example. Are they providing you with timely and relevant news that you need? Or are they constantly feeding you fear and entertainment packaged as news? Their messages affect us in ways we may not fully realize. We consume their content in the exact same way as we do a friend.

ACTION ITEMS

1) Curate your feed
Unfollow, unfriend, mute, and block *ruthlessly*. The same way an elite athlete protects their body from eating junk is the same way we need to protect our minds and hearts from consuming junk.

2) Cultivate relationships
Change your focus from accumulating more friends and followers to cultivating the relationships with the close friends you do have.

3) Watch what you share
Scroll back through your post history and take account of what you've posted and why. Look for instances where you may have overshared, or had an intention like showing off.

CHAPTER THREE

#PHONE

Maintaining all the new friendships and relationships enabled by social media means you have to engage them on the platforms they are on.

Prior to the digital age, maintaining friendships meant showing up to where your friends were. The neighborhood kids all played football in the street or basketball in the local park at around a particular time. If you wanted to play, you went and showed up. The local mall was a hangout spot, and going there on weekends meant running into friends. Sunday school and even family dinner parties on weekends served this function as well.

Showing up now looks quite a bit different. Instead of using a long commute home to call a friend to catch up, we now carry out asynchronous micro-conversations throughout the day. Engaging in friendship means replying to text messages, liking photos on social media, leaving comments, and then posting your own content for others to do the same.

The place to do all this is the phone. To avoid feeling left out, we become more and more dependent on our phones.

Think about how it felt to attend a wedding before the age of smartphones. You were forced to converse and make small talk with those seated at your table. Sometimes this was painstakingly boring, and other times it could serendipitously spark an important connection or relationship.

Constant engagement on the phone has created a trade-off in these casual social settings where we would normally meet new people. We converse less with those seated next to us on a plane, or with our barber, or even a fellow dinner guest at someone's home.

The phone has single-handedly transformed and challenged conventional social norms. I remember once in college, speaking to a brother at the masjid who was an international student. As our conversation went on for what felt like a long time, I casually glanced at my watch to check the time. He immediately became offended and asked me if he was wasting my time or keeping me from something urgent.

Responding to text messages while conversing with someone is now viewed by many to be completely normal and acceptable. Regardless, it does create some tricky social situations. When is it appropriate to respond to a message? Or glance at a message? What about taking a phone call? What about taking a picture?

Even beyond the phone, what about replying to these things on a smartwatch? Does that make a digital interaction more or less acceptable in varying settings?

These questions are not easily answered, and they will constantly evolve based on what society deems culturally acceptable. There are, however, certain teachings of the Prophet ﷺ that govern these interactions.

Imagine for a moment, two people in a group of three texting back and forth about the third person. It may seem harmless, and yet, we find guidance about these types of interactions in our tradition.

The Prophet ﷺ said, "When three people are sitting together, then two of them should not hold a secret conversation excluding the third person. Wait to be in a larger group so as not to upset the other person."[11]

This hadith is profound in demonstrating that no matter how much things change, the guidance covering the ethics of this type of communication already exists. Our tradition is timeless in the sense that its teachings will apply regardless of how communication methods may change.

It is narrated about the Prophet ﷺ that he faced the person he spoke to, with his chest and body. When he addressed someone, he completely turned his face towards that person and did not give a side glance.[12]

This hadith provides an understanding of good character in the digital age. When we are speaking to someone in person, we should not allow a digital device to detract our attention. This is especially true when it comes to close relationships such as family members – with a special emphasis on the respect given to our parents.

---

11 Bukhārī
12 *Shamāil Muhammadiyyah*

ACTION ITEMS

1) Look for creative ways to remove phones from social interactions. Many live shows (such as stand-up comedy) require audience members to lock their phones in a special pouch. Instead of selfie stations, host photo-free gatherings. One solution people have tried at restaurants is to stack phones at the center of the table, and if anyone reaches for their phone during dinner, they have to pay the full bill.

2) Force yourself to put your phone away when talking to others, even in casual settings like when speaking to a clerk at the store.

CHAPTER FOUR

#REFLECT

"[Those] who remember God standing, sitting, and lying down, who reflect on the creation of the heavens and earth: 'Our Lord! You have not created all this without purpose- You are far above that!- so protect us from the torment of the Fire."[13]

It's 30 minutes before *fajr* time ends. The alarm on your smartphone starts blaring. You reach over and try to swipe the screen but end up smacking your phone and hope it went into snooze mode. A few minutes later it goes off again. You're slightly aware that prayer time is ending soon and grab your phone. With one eye barely opened, and the other eye unable to open, you unlock the phone. The bright screen smacks you in the face.

Ding. 27 new emails. You quickly go through them to see if there's anything important. Even though they're all spam and it's been years since you received a personal email that you looked forward to, you still check them.

Blurry-eyed or not, your fingers instinctively go to your social media apps to go through your new notifications. Did any-

---

[13] 3:191

#REFLECT

one like the photo I posted last night? Who left comments and what do they say? Who are my new followers? Then we cycle through our group chats and catch up on all the latest arguments.

Eventually, you roll out of bed, and, oh yeah... that whole *fajr* thing.

The entire day is somewhat similar. Sit down and check work emails and personal emails. Check messages in work messaging apps like Slack or Teams, and then right back over to personal messages in WhatsApp or Telegram.

The drive home is the same thing. We check all our apps at red lights.

We do it while waiting in line at the store, or the drive-through at the coffee shop.

We are mentally exhausted by the time we arrive home. Our minds have been racing, and yet we accomplished nothing. Then we veg out by binge-watching episodes of a random show until it's time to go to bed.

At night, we repeat the same cycle, only putting the phone down after we're no longer afraid of having enough energy to stay awake - that is, being at the point of completely passing out.

Every wakeful moment we have is dedicated to being busy in some capacity.

We're *never* bored. And that's not necessarily a good thing. Social media is a tool, and each tool has trade-offs. Every interruption is rationalized. There are people we need to connect with, inquiries that demand our replies, and photos that need to be liked.

The question we need to consider is: What are the trade-offs of filling all of our free time with social media?

Author Michael Harris notes, "As we embrace a technology's gifts, we usually fail to consider what they ask from us in return—the subtle, hardly noticeable payments we make in exchange for their marvelous service. We don't notice, for example, that the gaps in our schedules have disappeared because we're too busy delighting in the amusements that fill them. We forget the games that childhood boredom forged because boredom itself has been outlawed. Why would we bother to register the end of solitude, of ignorance, of lack? Why would we care that an absence has disappeared?"[14]

In the pursuit to connect, we have given up our free time. We deplete our cognitive energy without giving it a chance to restore because we've eliminated whatever white space existed in our lives. We've lost the ability to be alone with our own thoughts and emotions.

In short, we have lost the ability to *reflect*.

"[This is] a blessed Book which We have revealed to you, [O Prophet], that they might reflect upon its verses and that those of understanding might take heed."[15]

The pursuit to connect makes us neglectful of our connection with Allah.

We must intentionally choose in every single moment which connections matter. When we choose to scroll through

---

14 *End of Absence*
15 38:29

our feeds until we fall asleep and then grab our phones the moment we wake up, we make *duā* a casualty of our digital lives.

We aren't able to give the remembrance of Allah the attention it needs because we dedicate our cognitive energy elsewhere.

When we no longer have downtime in our lives, we no longer have natural moments that spark reflection on the Creator.

Harris also notes, "Just as every technology is an invitation to enhance some part of our lives, it's also, necessarily, an invitation to be drawn away from something else."[16]

Awareness is critical. If we can't naturally find the moments to remember Allah, we have to engineer them. We have to create moments of solitude and reflection. *Duā* is not an item we can multitask. We have to create moments where we can pour our heart out to Allah with full attention - not partial attention.

Instead of squeezing in *dhikr* and *duā* when we find the time, those devotional acts must take priority over the other connections we make throughout the day.

We have to reclaim our expendable hours and make them hours essential to our connection with Allah.

---

16 *The End of Absence*

ACTION ITEMS

1) Reflect: What trade-offs have you made for social media? Have you noticed a direct impact on your relationship with Allah?

2) Block out timings throughout the day as "whitespace" that are screen-free. Suggestions include blocking the first 30 minutes after waking up, and 30 minutes before going to sleep.

3) Use a physical copy of the Qur'an (instead of an app) when reading, and use a hand-written *duā* list for making *duā*. These will eliminate distractions and help you focus.

CHAPTER FIVE

#Takathur

When I went to Disney World as a kid, my Dad would make us stop at major landmarks and pose for photos. We got the usual ones such as at Epcot, in front of the Magic Castle, and of course standing next to Mickey Mouse. Aside from that, we enjoyed the park like anyone else.

A trip to Disney now is quite different. People have their phones up taking videos of nearly every minute of the trip. They are posting photos while waiting in line. It almost feels like an uncomfortably long photo shoot as opposed to a fun day at the park.

Somewhere along the way we reached a tipping point where documenting an event became more important than actually experiencing it. Take a look at the crowd during a tense moment at any sporting event and you will see everyone with their phones out waiting to capture the next moment. The instant validation of posting a photo and receiving likes and comments further incentivizes the behavior to document instead of experience.

Allah says in Surah *al-Takāthur*, "Competition for more distracts you until you visit the graveyards."[17]

This ayah is traditionally understood as a warning against competing with others in regard to wealth and family. These are worldly forms of currency.

Social media adds a new form of currency – attention. This is measured in likes, comments, shares, and followers. We compete with one another over these metrics. The same way we label wealthy people as successful, we now do the same for those with large online followings.

There's a phrase, "keeping up with the Joneses," that means competing with your neighbor over material wealth. If they get a new car, you also go get a new car. Social media provides the same sentiment.

If we see someone post photos from a new park, we have to visit it and post a photo from the same spot. If a new restaurant opens up that is trending on social media, we rush to visit and take our photos before the hype dies down.

Sometimes the documentation can start with a noble intention and then become problematic. Consider the case of people documenting charity work such as feeding the homeless. It can serve as something that helps an organization build credibility, share the good work being done, and encourage support for the cause. Left unchecked, it can also become a source of self-adulation and shifting the focus from helping people to lauding the one doing the helping.

---

17 102:1-2

It is as if we are more motivated by the idea of documenting an experience than actually enjoying it. A family trip to Disney is no longer a fun experience. It is a photo shoot in which we document our activities to get likes. Instead of quality family time, it becomes a performance meant to project a certain family image to online followers.

True memories are made with a sentiment that comes from the emotion of an actual experience. It is those moments that you think about from a long time ago that make you smile.

ACTION ITEMS

1) Self-Reflection: Have you ever gone somewhere with the intent of taking a photo to share online instead of the experience of visiting that place?

2) Next time you visit a place or do something you would be tempted to document, focus on enjoying the moment without taking *any* photos (not even for personal memory).

CHAPTER SIX

#PUBLICIZINGSINS

"Indeed, those who like that immorality should be spread among the believers will have a painful punishment in this world and the Hereafter. Allah knows and you do not know."[18]

It's happened to pretty much everyone. You come across the online profile of an old friend or acquaintance and start clicking through the photos. And then you see it - your old Sunday School buddy chugging a beer.

The behavior itself is nothing new. Every son of Adam (as) is a sinner. People would do their best to cover up their behavior. If they were open with it, at the least, it was not widely spread. What social media has enabled is the speed and scale to which that sin is publicized. Even people who do not care to know about it see the photos pop up in their feeds.

Making matters worse is that publicizing of sins is something that builds clout on social media. Photos are posted, and then others like and comment on them, further incentivizing both the behavior and the sharing of it online.

---

18 24:19

The Prophet ﷺ said, "Everyone from my nation will be forgiven except those who sin in public. Among them is a man who commits an evil deed in the night that Allah has hidden for him. Then in the morning, he says, 'O people, I have committed this sin!' His Lord had hidden it during the night but in the morning, he reveals what Allah has hidden."[19]

One of the beautiful Names of Allah is *Al-Sittīr*. He is The One who loves to cover the sins of the servant. For someone to reject the mercy of their sin being covered and then publicize it is arrogantly rejecting the mercy of Allah. This is why the statement of the Prophet ﷺ here is so strict in indicating there is no forgiveness for those who publicize their sins. Instead of regret or guilt, they feel the need to boast.

There is a profound story narrated by Anas ibn Malik about a thief at the time of Umar. The thief said, "By Allah, I have never stolen before this." Umar said, "You have lied, by the Lord of Umar. Allah does not take a slave at the first sin." Then Alī ibn Abī Tālib said, "O Leader of the Believers, Allah is more forbearing than to take a slave for his first sin." Umar then gave the order and the man's hand was cut off. Then Alī asked him to speak the truth - how many times before had he stolen? He said, "21 times."[20]

The online world increases the propensity of sins becoming exposed. The people you follow, and the photos you like are public (even though some people do not realize it). Private mes-

---

19 Bukhārī and Muslim
20 AbdulMalik Mujahid, *Gems and Jewels*

sages, and even messages that disappear upon being viewed, can be easily screenshot or recorded. Even if we are not posting something ourselves, others may take and post photos of us without us realizing it.

The internet is forever.

This requires us to have an abundant sense of caution in our behavior. It means not only avoiding compromising situations, but also avoiding situations that could have the perception of it.

The example of the Prophet ﷺ was to avoid and clarify a situation that could cast doubt. Safiyya bint Huyayy tells us that while the Prophet ﷺ was in *i'tikāf*, she came to visit him and speak with him. When she stood up to go back, he did as well to say good-bye. As this happened, two people from the Ansar happened to pass by. When they saw the Prophet ﷺ, they began to walk swiftly, and he said, "Walk calmly, she is Safiyya bint Huyayy [my wife]... Both of them said: Messenger, subhanAllah, (we cannot conceive of anything doubtful even in the remotest corners of our minds), whereupon he said, 'Satan circulates in the body of man just as blood circulates, and I was afraid he would instill evil suspicion in your hearts."[21]

Beyond the spiritual impact, there are worldly consequences to this type of behavior. It is not uncommon for people to have college admissions, scholarships, employment opportunities, and even marriage proposals negatively impacted due to something they posted on social media.

---

21 Muslim

Despite these consequences, people continue to post this type of material. Social media is designed in a way that encourages and incentivizes that behavior. The advertising adage of "sex sells" holds up, as does the journalism saying "if it bleeds, it leads."

Vincent Cerf, known as one of the "fathers of the internet" commented, "The internet is a reflection of our society and that mirror is going to be reflecting what we see. If we do not like what we see in that mirror the problem is not to fix the mirror, we have to fix society."

The same content gets attention online, and attention yields clout or influence.

Even when we do not share our own misdeeds online, it is tempting to share what others have done. This enables a vulture culture type of environment where we turn our social media feeds into the tabloids at the supermarket. We hone in on the mistakes of others so we can spread them.

The Prophet ﷺ said, "O you who have believed with their tongues yet faith has not entered their hearts! Do not back-bite the Muslims, and do not seek to discover their faults, for whoever seeks after their faults, Allah will seek his faults. And if Allah seeks his faults, He will expose him even (what he committed) in his home."[22]

When the metrics of success are oriented around engagement (likes, shares, comments), then we are automatically incentivized to post content that succeeds on those metrics. This

---

22 Abu Dawūd

is magnified further when society rewards people who do this outside the world of social media. Many famous celebrities and influencers initially obtained fame from doing something lewd or immoral. Once they attained that fame, they were able to leverage it into business empires encompassing reality TV shows, fashion lines, and A-list celebrity status. This creates a blueprint for others to follow – a shortcut to fame and success.

Of course, this type of fame comes at the cost of compromising our morals. The Prophet ﷺ said, "If you feel no shame, do as you wish."[23]

Covering our sins when every digital tool we utilize encourages us to expose them is challenging to say the least.

One reason people fall into this trap is the immediate sense of validation received from the attention. It is vital for people to invest in developing higher-quality relationships at home and with close friends. True good companionship is a safeguard against the anonymous validation social media provides.

One element of good companionship laid out by the Prophet ﷺ is the concealment of one another's mistakes – "A Muslim is a Muslim's brother: he does not wrong him or abandon him. If anyone cares for his brother's need, Allah will care for his need; if anyone removes a Muslim's anxiety, Allah will remove from him, on account of it, one of the anxieties of the Day of resurrection; and if anyone conceals a Muslim's fault, Allah will conceal his fault on the Day of Resurrection."[24]

---

23 Bukhārī
24 Abu Dawūd

ACTION ITEMS

Learn and make this duā regularly:

O Allah, I ask You for pardon and well being in this life and the next. O Allah, I ask You for pardon and well-being in my religious and worldly affairs, and my family and my wealth. O Allah, veil (*sitr*) my weaknesses and set at ease my dismay. O Allah, preserve me from the front and from behind and on my right and on my left and from above, and I take refuge with You lest I be swallowed up by the earth.[25]

---

25 Abu Dawūd, al-Nasa'ī, Ibn Mājah, and al-Bukhārī (in al-Adab al-Mufrad) report from Abdullah ibn Umar that the Prophet ﷺ would never fail to make these supplications every morning and evening.

CHAPTER SEVEN

#Family

The introduction of the smartphone has created a litany of unprecedented challenges for the family.

We have gone from a family culture where the house phone is not answered during dinner time, to everyone eating at the same table while staring at their own screen.

There are questions for which we have no blueprint – what age should kids be allowed to use screens? Get their own phone?

Work-life balance has been obliterated for some. The phone creates an always-on and always-available environment. This makes it difficult for those with high demanding jobs, or businesses to run, to balance time between work and family.

Parents and children alike blame each other for spending too much time on their screens. Many complain that weeks and months go by of a family physically living in the same home, but all leading different (digital) lives.

Day to day family life is not particularly exciting when you think about it. Everyone has to wake up to get to school or work. Breakfast must be served, lunches packed, and dishes put away. Then there is the vacuuming, the laundry, and other chores. A family dinner and an hour of recreation such as a game night are often the most exciting parts of an average day. By the time those are done, everyone is exhausted and it is time to go to bed and do everything all over again.

On the other hand, our phones are *always* exciting. There is always a funny video to watch. There is always a fascinating debate happening in our group chats. There are funny pictures that need our witty comments. There are people saying things about Islam that are wrong on the internet, and so we jump to do the important work of correcting them.

It's not just that our phones are entertaining, they're also an escape. In my experience teaching Fiqh of Social Media seminars, I came across two consistent complaints. One was from women complaining about their husbands, and one from college age children complaining about their fathers. In both cases, the men led busy lives at work and would spend the entire evening at home zoned out chatting with friends on WhatsApp. It is an extreme level of being physically present but mentally and emotionally absent.

Without any intentional effort to control our usage of digital devices in the home, the default is that they will occupy all of our time and attention.

This effort requires a family coming to an understanding on a number of issues specific to social media usage.

What is family business?

Every family should have agreed upon rules regarding what can and cannot be shared.

A good starting point is an agreement not to share anything negative on social media. Spouses should not speak ill of each other online. Parents should not complain about their kids – and vice versa. Social media is not the place to air dirty laundry or even frustrations with family.

Our religion places such a heavy emphasis on maintaining family ties that it forces us to act with an abundance of caution regarding what we post. A post made in frustration can come back to cause harm even after an issue is resolved. Passive-aggressive posts (where frustration is aired without specifying it was an issue with family) will inevitably do the same.

Imagine a parent venting about their children to blow off steam. The child then sees this post the next day. Even if the issue between them was resolved, it will create a lingering negative impact. The child may, for example, become hesitant to share things with their parents out of fear of it being posted later on social media.

Consider a child trying to show their parents something only to get "wait 2 minutes" in response. Now consider that this is what happens every time a child tries to get their parent's attention over the course of 10 years. They will be conditioned to think that whoever is on the other side of the screen is more important. Many times, the relationship between parents and children breaks down not because of a singular catastrophic event, but erosion over time.

Similarly, children should be respectful of their parents. Responding to the call of your parents should always take priority over the email or message you are responding to – whether you are a child, or whether you are an adult with elderly parents.

The value and priority we give to our family is shown through small actions. We must push back against the urgent nature of social media and carefully assess the impacts of small actions on our families.

The types of photographs we post need ground rules as well. For example, it is wise to make sure no personally identifying information is accidentally put into a photograph. This includes things like license plates on your cars, the names of your kids' schools, or your home address.

Permission should be sought before posting a photo of someone else. In the case of minor children, this is even more important. It is not fair to them to create a digital trail of their lives that is publicly accessible without their input.

Good family business is also something to be cautious of. Marriage in particular is something that can cause envy or invite outside interference. Document the good memories for private reflection, not public consumption. The more that good memories are shared publicly in a relationship, the more that it invites opinions and comments, and also creates pressure to do and post more.

It is important to note that if someone is in a home where abuse of any type is occurring, they should immediately seek help from a qualified individual. The emphasis on maintaining family privacy should not be used to shame people into staying silent about harm that may be occurring to them.

Screen Limits

This is the toughest to manage, and the one without any easy rules of thumb. How much is each person allowed to use screens in a day?

The most important thing is for a family to come to an agreement, and then enforce it. It is okay if it changes or is a work in progress, as long as everyone remains on the same page.

In establishing this policy, it is important to consider a number of factors. With children, what do you consider to be a healthy amount of screen time? Under what circumstances can they get screens?

If you are inclined to limit screen usage, how do you then account for children feeling left out because their friends have access to them?

There are no easy answers to any of these questions. Some families will opt to limit screens to a set amount of daily time. Others will only allow them after a list of other things are done first (e.g. read Qur'an, clean your room, finish homework). Some may allow screens only on weekends. The route you choose depends largely on your own family dynamics, the maturity level of your children, and the level of trust you have with them.

Families should also consider creating screen-free times or screen-free zones. For example, it could be a household rule that screens are not allowed at the dinner table. A husband and wife may agree to block out an hour every evening to spend time together without any screens. Some families do device round-ups by collecting all phones and tablets at a specified time such as 9 pm.

Relationships must be managed in addition to screens. Families should know who is connected to who. When kids are playing games online, who are they playing with, and who is able to send them messages?

Parents should have passwords to all accounts. This may sound like an infringement of privacy, but the potential harms of unknown people communicating with children is far too great to risk this. A case can be made that spouses should also have the passwords to each other's phones and accounts. This is a safeguard against both temptations and becoming doubtful of each other.

Families should be intentional about defining what quality time looks like for them, and how they can do it regularly. It may be going to the park or going for a walk. It may very well be playing video games together. Identify what works for your family, and then make a plan and stick to it.

The trap to avoid is comparing your family life to someone else's. Every family has a different situation.

ACTION ITEMS

1) Call a family meeting and walk through the issues raised here. What does healthy screen time and social media engagement look like for your family, and how will you follow through on it?

2) Identify screen-free family times. To start out, try either a screen-free dinner time or no screens allowed after 8 pm.

Approach these with the mindset of experimentation. You may try something, and after 2 weeks you realize it is not working. No problem, meet again and adjust. This will be a constantly evolving process.

CHAPTER EIGHT

#ENVY

The Prophet ﷺ said, "Envy is permitted only in two cases: A man whom Allah gives wealth, and he disposes of it rightfully, and a man to whom Allah gives knowledge which he applies and teaches it."[26]

Consuming social media can elicit any number of reactions depending on the content. We laugh when we see something funny, feel sad when we read bad news, or even outrage when we see something offensive. These are temporary and pass as we scroll through our feeds.

Envy, however, settles in the heart and does not go away easily. It festers. And it can be destructive.

We all have tough days. We all have days where we are under a lot of stress at work and it feels like there is no way out. We can feel overwhelmed with responsibilities at school or at home. Sometimes we are flat out going through a rough patch where it really seems nothing is going in our favor.

The phone is a convenient coping mechanism. We blow off some steam by scrolling through social media. And we often

---

26 Bukhārī and Muslim

see exactly those things that are the opposite of the difficulty we are facing.

The person having difficulty getting married opens up social media only to see newlywed couples posting pictures from their honeymoon with a heart drawn in the sand on the beach and their toes pointing to the ocean.

The person stuck in a dead-end job with a difficult manager sees others posting about getting promoted at work despite lacking in qualification. The one who struggled to pay rent on time this month sees photos of friends enjoying exotic vacations abroad. The couple struggling to conceive sees a flurry of pictures and videos of cute babies.

Social media is designed to curate and promote highlights. We post the best snapshots of our days, the best meals we eat, and the best places we visit. When you have a stretch of a tough few days, it can be easy to feel like everyone else has it easy and only you are dealing with this type of difficulty.

It creates a type of insecurity. A person starts to wonder why they cannot get things together when it appears to be so easy. Online marketing is designed to exploit exactly these types of insecurities.

When people are struggling with, for example, a difficult work situation, they will become more attuned to messaging around that issue. They will notice more posts around following your passions, lifestyle entrepreneurship, finding a dream job, resume hacks, or general motivational quotes.

As they progress down that path, more and more products claiming to solve this problem will reach them via targeted advertising. These products will have testimonials from people just like them showing that it is possible. Over time, it will feel like everyone else is succeeding. This is when resentment and envy take root in the heart.

Why is it so easy for everyone else, but so difficult for me?

The illusion of being immediately attainable is there because we only see the success stories. This is also known as survivorship bias. The stories of failure never reach us. And not all the success we see is actually success. Many online influencers stage photoshoots with rented exotic cars, or small studios staged to look like private planes.

To look at this from a completely different perspective, consider the Ramadan experience. During that month, our social media feeds are full of people cooking special traditional meals with full table spreads. People are posting photos of reconnecting with friends and large family gatherings. We see the people posting daily from the masjid, and then during *i'tikāf* as well. Families post stunningly perfect photographs of their meticulously done Ramadan décor.

For the person working long hours, or exhausted from chasing around small children, or the one with no friends or family to celebrate with, it can be spiritually draining. It is easy to consume that content and feel that your Ramadan is not up to par.

The danger of envy that social media magnifies is that it pits us against our peers. If we see a famous scholar posting about their Ramadan experience it is something we can admire from afar. It is when we see people similar to us – other parents just like us, other working professionals like us – that we feel envy. That is when we feel stressed. There is more pressure to be perfect, because my friend who is just like me appears to be doing it, so why can't I?

Sometimes these feelings develop out of simply not feeling included. We see friends out together and start to wonder why we were not invited as well. This can cause a person to feel forgotten or neglected.

After feeling like this, we then feel guilty about how we feel because we know it is not a productive emotion. Intellectually we understand that everything is by the decree of Allah and we should not question it. In practice, however, it is difficult to not feel envy, resentment, or sadness. This is because it feels like we deserve, are entitled to, or just *should* be successful in exactly the way we desire.

Our inclination to view material blessings as a sign of self-worth or a sign of Allah's love is highlighted in the Qur'an, "[The nature of] man is that, when his Lord tries him through honor and blessings, he says, 'My Lord has honored me,' but when He tries him through the restriction of his provision, he says, 'My Lord has humiliated me.'"[27]

This is a problem that comes from the challenge of knowing what Islam says but struggling to implement it. Interestingly, philosopher Alain de Botton commented, "The other thing about modern society and why it causes this anxiety, is that we have nothing at its center that is non-human. We are the first

---

27 89:15-16

society to be living in a world where we don't worship anything other than ourselves. We think very highly of ourselves, and so we should; we've put people on the Moon, done all sorts of extraordinary things. And so we tend to worship ourselves. Our heroes are human heroes. That's a very new situation. Most other societies have had, right at their center, the worship of something transcendent."

Seeking the acceptance of Allah instead of the validation of people is a profound shift in mindset. When we obsess about feeling good or feeling successful by the same metrics as we see on social media, we actually become obsessed with our own selves – i.e., ego. We seek to be accepted in a place where only the extraordinary highlights are broadcast.

This comes when we recalibrate our success metrics away from social media and other people to earning the pleasure of Allah.

The Prophet ﷺ said about a person, "If he is striving to provide for his young children then he is considered to be in the path of Allah. If he is striving to provide for his elderly parents, then he is considered to be in the path of Allah. And if he is striving to provide for himself to avoid being dependent on others then he is considered to be in the path of Allah."[28]

This gives us a better way of looking at the struggles we face with something like a career. Instead of the daily grind overwhelming us and making us feel stressed and anxious, it allows us to reframe it in our minds as a struggle that is pleasing to

---

28 Tabarani

Allah even while we pray to Him to open new doors of opportunity for us.

The Prophet ﷺ said, "Look at those who have less than you and do not look at those who are above you, for that will make you more inclined to not reject the favors of Allah."[29]

ACTION ITEMS

1) Set realistic expectations for yourself based on your circumstances. Make *duā* to Allah and rely on Him for a way out of your difficulties. In the context of envy, become regular in making *duā* to Allah to bless the good you see in others, and to alleviate the difficulties you see others going through.

2) Ensure that your online time is coupled with time to develop meaningful relationships offline. It is through these relationships that you can remind yourself no one has it easy, and your friends are struggling as well (even if their particular struggle is different from yours). These friends are also an important source of support.

3) Remember that what you post online may be something that causes envy in others. Be mindful of the good news you share and how it may affect those who are struggling.

4) If you find yourself feeling envy toward others, make *duā* that Allah blesses them, and also blesses you. *Shaytān* will stop casting it in your heart when he sees it as counterproductive.

---

29 ibn Mājah

CHAPTER NINE

#CHANGE

How do you feel about social media activism? Is it a real thing, or is it just a trick we play on ourselves to make us think we're actually doing something good for a cause? And how much good does it actually do?

This was an email sent to me via my email list. The answers are: I'm cautious about it, it depends, and probably not as much as we think it does.

There is no question that social media influences viewpoints and behaviors. That is what makes it such a powerful tool. What you consume online influences your purchasing decisions, diet, parenting style, study habits, religious views, personal finance, political views, friendships, vacation destinations, and literally everything else in your life.

Does this tool also work the other way? Can I do something on an individual level to change someone else's mind about something?

It certainly feels like we *should* be able to. This is why we invest so much time trying to change other people's minds. Our back and forth debates over group texts or in the comments section on a friend's post are ultimately trying to get someone else to see things differently than they currently do.

The more that others participate in online activism, the more pressure mounts for you to also participate. After a tragedy, it is not uncommon for people to update their profile picture to a flag representing the affected country as a show of solidarity.

It is a simple and effortless action. And that's the trap.

If you do not update your picture, you are now accountable to the suspicions of others. Do you not care about this cause? Why do you feel affected by other tragedies, but cannot even be bothered to show solidarity for this one? Are you not sympathetic? Don't you realize that you could help spread awareness? Why didn't you add your email address to the online petition?

Now you have to either justify saying no, or go ahead and do it. Most choose the latter, although they don't see how this activism makes a difference. It's just an easier option than trying to justify *not* doing it. We fake a "social consciousness" to keep up with our friends.

This is what gets labeled as *performative activism* or *virtue signaling*.

Social media has created a culture that rewards people for wanting to be known as the type of person who cares about a cause more than for actually caring about it.

This is why people do things like share articles without reading them. It conveys a certain type of image of who the person is. In a situation of tragedy, social media feeds the ego and makes the suffering of others another reason to bring focus back on yourself. What does it say *about me* to update my profile picture, or contribute to this cause, or share this article, or amplify a particular voice?

Digging deeper, is our concern for a cause driven by compassion, or a self-serving desire to take part in something that is going viral and will result in attention?

An obvious question that gets missed is – what is the point? What is the desired outcome? What is the net positive impact of "awareness"? The truth is these things cannot be measured in any meaningfully quantifiable manner.

These are tough questions that require significant introspection and assessment of one's own intentions.

Sincerity is shown by what is done offline. Have you contributed financially? Have you volunteered any time to go do some type of work on the ground? How much *duā* did you make regarding a particular cause? Did you wake up at night and pray for those affected?

Unfortunately, actions like *duā* are devalued or made out to be a last resort – all our actions have failed, so now we turn to duā. When a believer sincerely cares for something, the *first* thing they should do is call out to Allah for help. That prayer may very well be coupled with some type of action online. Social media activism without the element of prayer, however, is a telling sign of self-serving action and virtue signaling.

When we are entrapped by the currency of social media (attention), we evaluate our actions based upon that metric.

The impact of online activism then is not measured in lives changed, but by numbers of views.

Accepting that premise and acting upon it has its own consequences. The cause we are advocating for is now competing against other causes in the marketplace for attention. We see this most commonly displayed with "whataboutery" – when someone posts something about one cause, another inevitably replies saying "well what about this other cause?"

This is a passive-aggressive way to undermine advocacy for one cause in favor of another. A person may say "pray for Palestine" and someone replies "but what about praying for Syria?" This sentiment is born when we are competing for attention, and feel we need attention to win.

We want our cause to beat out the other causes: The human suffering attached to my cause outranks the human suffering attached to your cause. I have to make sure people's thoughts, prayers, and compassion are directed at my cause. If they go to your cause, none will be left for mine. My cause has to get all the clicks.

In this manner, we engage in "moral point-scoring" with our online activism. We win points by simultaneously promoting our cause, and tearing down the causes others support. This results in the shaping of our discourse. We move away from informed analysis to hot takes. We form more and more extreme talking points to get more people to talk about our thing instead of the other one.

We feel compelled to speak on and have an opinion about every issue we see in our feeds. Silence is taken as opposition to a cause. Whenever anyone speaks, we worry more about all the issues they neglect rather than paying attention to the human impact of what they're actually saying.

Online activism becomes less and less about helping those in need, and more and more about policing who is speaking about issues and in what manner. We sit at our computers waiting to be told what to care about next. This turns some people into outrage junkies. They thrive on creating an online commotion every time something happens.

This runs directly contrary to the advice of our Prophet ﷺ who said, "There will be afflictions (in the near future) during which a sitting person will be better than a standing one, and the standing one will be better than the walking one, and the walking one will be better than the running one, and whoever will expose himself to these afflictions, they will destroy him. So whoever can find a place of protection or refuge from them, should take shelter in it."[30]

When we continue to dive headfirst into every issue we see online, it will become mentally exhausting. The sheer magnitude of issues one could (or should) care about becomes overwhelming. So when the internet tries to make you care about everything, you end up caring about nothing.

Compassion fatigue sets in. We feel guilty and overwhelmed.

At some point, we come to realize that the causes we are advocating for are big problems that need big solutions. We know we cannot sustain empathy for everything. Ideally, this would

---

30 Bukhārī

lead us to becoming more selective, or focusing our energy on those issues where we have an emotional connection or some other type of vested interest.

There is a slightly sinister side (depending on how you look at it) to how social media shapes what you care about.

> *"Mark Zuckerberg, a journalist was asking him a question about the news feed. And the journalist was asking him, "Why is this so important?" And Zuckerberg said, "A squirrel dying in your front yard may be more relevant to your interests right now than people dying in Africa." And I want to talk about what a Web based on that idea of relevance might look like."*[31] *-Eli Pariser*

The social media companies decide, for example, which tragedies will provide the option of updating your profile picture in solidarity. As we consume content about one issue, or similar types of issues, algorithms then kick in. They note our interest, and then continue to serve up similar content.

Without realizing it, we are in the ultimate echo chamber. Everyone we know is talking about the same thing and from the same point of view. It is then unfathomable for anyone to *not* take part, or have a differing opinion. Any difference of opinion becomes marginalized by the mob of people I follow, or by the algorithms at play.

Activism then becomes an act of intolerance. We are not able to deal with anyone who thinks differently, or does not

---

31 Filter Bubbles

act in exactly the same way we do in advocacy of a particular cause.

Moreover, we assume that if people simply saw the things we saw, they would think the way we think. Hours are then invested into debates over group text and comments sections sharing and resharing the content that supports our views while ignoring everything else.

The examples we see of successful social media activism and mobilization can set unrealistic expectations. People think that posting something to 100 strangers or 20 friends is going to somehow completely counteract the effects of the politico-media complex. When it doesn't, it's a failure. Then we move on to the next thing and try again.

To understand effective social media activism it is important to distinguish between Big Social and Small Social. Most people are shooting for Big Social. They want their message to be seen by 10 million people and magically change their minds. They want their cool comment with the appropriate hashtag to somehow get picked up by the news ticker on a cable news channel and make their viewers see the light.

That's not going to happen.

What people can do instead is focus on affecting their more personal networks. These are people you have deeper relationships with – people who will not be fooled by your virtue signaling or performative activism. These are people you can have frank discussions with and challenge each other's views. Social media can be utilized as a great tool to facilitate those discussions.

The ultimate irony here is that effective social media activism is focused on those people you already have a strong relationship with built over time - not the thousands of extended connections you're trying to reach at the speed of light (which is what social media incentivizes).

The Prophetic perspective is to take a long-term approach. Anas ibn Malik reported that the Prophet ﷺ said, "If the Resurrection were established upon one of you while he has in his hand a sapling, then let him plant it."[32]

Do your part purposefully and intentionally, and know that Allah will take care of the results. The instant validation and metrics of social media can give the illusion of making us feel as if we are in control of the results.

Adopt a mindset of planting seeds. Diligently do the necessary work that lays a foundation even if you will not see the results yourself.

---

32 Musnad Ahmad

ACTION ITEMS

1) Self-assessment: Have you tried to raise awareness for an issue online but neglected making *duā* for it? Remedy this by making *duā* for those causes you advocate for.

2) The next time an issue goes viral that you do not have a directly vested interest in, remain silent about it on social media and see what the effects are on you personally.

3) Carve out time to have a meaningful conversation with a friend if you have different perspectives on an issue – approach it with the intent of understanding their viewpoint as opposed to trying to express your own.

CHAPTER TEN

#EchoChambers

In 2008, a social media "controversy" erupted about Barack Obama being Muslim. The number of Americans who believed this doubled *after* the election – and this increase happened mostly among college-educated people.

Why would so many seemingly smart people believe something that was *clearly* not true?

People tend to consume content from people they identify with. Conservatives will follow the same channels, and liberals another. We see the same with Islamic ideologies. People consume content from scholars they feel the most connection to.

A person may read an article online and "like" it. The algorithms developed by social media companies pick this up and start suggesting other articles on the issue from similar media outlets. This person then goes on social media where they follow talking heads with the same worldview, unsurprisingly expressing the same opinions. This is then reinforced again by what they see for hours on cable news and other videos online. This content consumption is followed by conversations with friends who also share the same general views, and who share the same types of articles.

After all of this, a person will legitimately feel that the conclusion they have reached is an *informed opinion*. They have researched it, read up on it, and gone deep on this topic. This gives the feeling that it is a sound, accurate, and truthful take.

Algorithms are continually optimized to predict what type of content you like to consume so they can serve it up to you. This is why after you watch a video, the algorithm automatically displays videos enjoyed by people who liked that particular video. Online shopping sites do the same after you purchase something. While helpful for entertainment and online purchases, it requires caution when it comes to information consumption. Your identity informs the media you receive, and the media you receive further shapes your identity.

This is why people become more and more extreme in their views. It feels impossible to accept any other views as grounded in reality when it overwhelmingly feels like your views are correct. You are never exposed (by design) to any information that will challenge your viewpoints, only those that reinforce them. The more extreme your views become, the more difficult it is to empathize with anyone who thinks differently. No longer able to grapple with different views, we retreat back to our bubbles to seek comfort. Thus, the echo chamber is born.

Our information consumption needs to be monitored in the same way as our dietary consumption. We have a baseline understanding of what good nutrition is versus junk food. Unfortunately, we do not have the same understanding with our information diet.

Much of the media we consume has only a façade of informing and educating. In reality, it is entertainment designed to keep audiences captivated. Their business models incentivize them to produce content that gets attention, not content that leaves a positive impact. Hence the famous saying, if it bleeds, it leads.

> "If traffic ends up guiding coverage," The Washington Post's ombudsman writes, "will The Post choose not to pursue some important stories because they're 'dull?'" Will an article about, say, child poverty ever seem hugely personally relevant to many of us...?[33]

Important things are often boring, so they are not covered, nor are they shared virally on social media. When media companies are incentivized by traffic-driven monetization, and individuals are driven by attention-driven metrics – then it becomes nearly impossible to advance important ideas that do not quickly cause an emotional and viral reaction.

This works its way into Islamic discourse online. Debates over ideological issues and legal rulings will gain attention. Reminders to pray regularly with concentration will never go viral.

Our echo chambers also focus our attention. Certain causes, or crises, will go viral. Everyone is then expected to pay atten-

---

33 Eli Pariser, *Filter Bubbles*

tion to these topics. The problem which arises is that when we move from crisis to crisis, we lose the ability to see any type of bigger picture. We are not able to develop any type of principled focus or long-term care and advocacy.

Issues are simply not presented in a way that is even meant to inform, mitigate, or solve. They are only presented to incite emotions (such as outrage) that generate more online chatter and occupy attention.

We consume all this content online under the illusion of staying informed, or even learning. We participate in discussions hoping to affect change in some manner. The algorithms at play, however, manipulate our attention to focusing on issues chosen by others and retreat into a carefully crafted universe online made just for you, one that defines your own reality, without any context of a larger picture.

Consuming information we agree with is easy. Consuming information that challenges us is more difficult. Learning does not happen when we only take in content that conforms to all of our pre-existing views and opinions.

Learning occurs when we are presented with an information gap. We have to come across something we do not know or understand. It could be engaging a co-worker or colleague on a topic and having to sit and hear what they have to say rather than shunning the conversation and seeking refuge with like-minded friends on social media.

Learning requires the humility to know that what you think about a particular issue may be wrong, and finding ways to empathize with those who hold different views. This does not mean we should always seek out the contrarian view on everything, but we do need a healthy dose of alternative information to better ground ourselves and break the echo chambers.

When you find yourself going down a rabbit hole on an issue, look for reputable people that are dissimilar to you in terms of views and life experience. Follow them and read their content so you can understand the thought process by which people arrive at conclusions different from yours. Ultimately, this will either strengthen your views or make you realize you are incorrect about something.

A good example of this would be something like Islamic home financing. Many people have already made up their minds about the legitimacy or illegitimacy of these companies from an Islamic perspective. If this is an issue of concern to you, seek out reputable scholars who may even disagree with each other, and take some time to learn more deeply about the subject.

Seeking out reputable people is one part of verifying the information we consume and share.

> "O you who believe, if a troublemaker brings you news, check it first, in case you wrong others unwittingly and later regret what you have done."[34]

---

34 49:6

ACTION ITEMS

1) Seek out conversations with people who differ from you. Different upbringings, backgrounds, ethnicities, and so on. Those conversations need to be with the sincere intention of getting to know someone else, and where they are coming from.

2) Diversify your content consumption. Identify the areas of interest most pertinent to you, and go deeper on them. Work on developing a radar of sorts to identify when people are simply being partisan and unfollow them (even if they reinforce what you already believe).

3) Stop and reflect. Sometimes we are more in need of cutting consumption altogether than we are diversifying. When you feel like you are being taken on a ride, unfollow and mute relentlessly.

4) Become regular in making the Prophetic supplication, "O Allah, Lord of *Jibrīl*, *Mikā'īl* and *Isrāfīl,* Creator of the heavens and the earth, Knower of the unseen and the seen, You judge between Your slaves concerning wherein they differ. O Allah, guide me to the disputed matters of truth for You are the One Who guides to the Straight Path."[35]

5) Verify what you read, and verify what you share. Sometimes a quick internet search of the source is enough to alert you to potentially incorrect information. Pause and double-check your information before hitting the send or forward button to friends and family. Remember that the Prophet ﷺ warned us, "It is enough for a person to be guilty of lying if he relates everything that he hears."[36]

---

35 Nasa'ī
36 Reported by Muslim in the introduction of his Sahih.

CHAPTER ELEVEN

#NASIHAH

The Prophet ﷺ said, "The religion is sincerity (naṣīḥah)."[37] Every time we open our phones we see opportunities to advise. We see people posting misinformation, forwarding chain-letter types of messages to group chats, proclaiming religious opinions that may be incorrect, or simply acting in a way online that is inappropriate.

Having a conversation with someone about any of these actions is difficult. It is further complicated depending on who it is. What if that person is a family member? Employee? Superior? Community leader? Friend? Total stranger?

In some cases, we have a more direct responsibility to advise than others. When done correctly, *naṣīḥah* can be a beautiful action that leads to someone rectifying a mistake.

Done incorrectly, and you can tear apart family relationships, business relationships, and destroy friendships - all because you alienated someone by *how* you corrected them.

The art of delivering feedback has been lost in our community. We see less of a balanced approach and more of people

---

[37] Muslim

moving to one of two extremes – rude and in-your-face bluntness, or complete apathy.

Applying the golden rule here would dictate that we give advice the same way we want to receive it. This is a good way to guide our discussion, but it needs more context for the online world.

Receiving critical feedback is uncomfortable. No matter how much we try to rise above our own ego, it still stings when someone calls us out for doing something wrong.

Effectively delivering feedback means *creating an environment* in which the recipient can take feedback, reflect on it, and learn from it.

The intention behind correcting someone is crucial. Do you sincerely want the other person to become better as a result of this advice? That shapes what you say, how you say it, how you prepare, and how you follow up on it. For example, did you stop and actually make *duā* for the betterment of the person before giving them advice? Did you make *duā* for them to be able to implement it after delivering it?

Too often, in the age of social media, delivering advice has become a type of performance art to display "righteous outrage" at some transgression. "Advice" is delivered in public forums not for the betterment of the individual, but for virtue-signaling or pandering.

Delivering advice effectively is built upon a relationship of trust.

> "How well you take criticism depends less on the message and more on your relationship with the messenger. It's surprisingly easy to hear a hard truth when it comes from someone who believes in your potential and cares about your success." -Adam Grant

The manner with which a parent can correct their own child is drastically different from how we would correct a stranger at the masjid. What is your relationship and level of trust with a person?

When we misread that relationship, it creates negative consequences. Calling someone out online, especially if you don't have a personal relationship, will most likely result in them getting defensive and doubling down. In this case, "advising" a person has created a greater evil than the one it was trying to stop.

They have, as the Prophet ﷺ warned, "helped the devil against their brother."[38]

Once a relationship of trust exists, the actual art of delivering feedback will vary based on circumstance. Sometimes it may be candid and immediate. Sometimes it will require patience and gentleness.

Sometimes your advice may take a long time to have any effect, and sometimes it won't have any at all.

The question you have to ask yourself is whether your presence in someone's life is decreasing or increasing their motivation to change?

---

38 Bukhārī

If it is the latter, then it means you have to keep your eye on the long term. Social media fosters a "cancel culture" where corrective action must be both immediate and public. When someone messes up, there is immense pressure to not only apologize, but do so in the exact manner being demanded.

Unfortunately, due to the attention driven metrics of social media, the patience required of long-term relationship building is not incentivized. Instead of advice, we get continuous cycles of outrage. Instead of reaching out to people directly, we get reaction videos to ridicule them instead.

Instead of advice being about rectification or betterment, it devolves into a type of point-scoring with people competing to outdo one another in displaying their moral righteousness.

The internet can make us forget we are dealing with real people. The potential of our messages reaching hundreds of thousands of people imbues a false sense of self-importance into our actions.

This shifts the discourse away from a default of kindness to one of cruelty. Wisdom and gentleness are replaced with harshness and a reckless abandon for telling the truth like it is.

The Prophet ﷺ said, "Verily, gentleness is not found in anything but that it beautifies it, and it is not removed from anything but that it disgraces it."[39]

Social media does not incentivize kindness in the same way it does notoriety. When people immerse themselves online, they come across a lot of things. It is not uncommon to see

---

39 Muslim

Muslims spreading misinformation or engaging in openly *haram* behavior. The more a person consumes this content, the more it looks like *everyone* is like this. It feels like a bad case of the emperor with no clothes.

So they overreact and go to the other extreme.

They see others watering down the religion, or treating it carelessly, so they feel it is their obligation to do the opposite. Others who feel the same way give them instant validation on social media by liking and resharing these comments. This reaction is perceived to be defending the truth, and being authentic. Thus, the echo chamber thus gets louder and louder.

Alī said, "There are three types of people: (1) the Godly scholar who acts upon what he knows, (2) the seeker of knowledge upon the path of salvation, and (3) the chaotic mobs that follow everyone who calls out and are carried like the wind - they did not enlighten themselves with the light of [true] knowledge, nor did they refer back to a reliable source."[40]

The Prophet ﷺ said, "There shall come upon people years of deceit in which the liar will be believed, the truthful one disbelieved, the treacherous will be trusted, the trustworthy one considered treacherous, and the *Ruwaybidah* shall speak out.' It was said: Who are the *Ruwaybidah*? The Prophet ﷺ said: 'The lowly, contemptible one who will speak out about public affairs.'"[41]

When this happens, proving yourself correct on an issue takes priority over actually rectifying the belief or action of

---

40 *Hilyatu'l-Awliya*
41 Ibn Mājah

the other person. This is a subtle but consequential shift. It removes sincerity from the equation and puts the ego at the forefront. The discussion is done under a façade of *dawah* but results in attention that can only be described as self-serving. The only people who celebrate it are ones that already agree with it. It builds a following instead of relationships, and is therefore unable to accomplish the ultimate task of winning hearts and minds or changing someone's viewpoint.

In fact, it can do the opposite. While such a person may find much fanfare online, their interactions in real life may be drastically different. Someone who constantly calls out others belligerently at the masjid or a social gathering would be insufferable.

The work of building a relationship that fosters an environment for advice to be accepted and for people to willingly change their behavior or views requires long-term relationship building.

We rarely, if ever, change something based on reading an anonymous comment online. We only change after conversations with trusted friends or exploring an issue in-depth.

If we truly want to help people better themselves, then we must take on the difficult task of community building. It can be done online, but it requires a shift in approach. Where social media incentivizes the short-game, meaningful change requires looking at the long-game.

When the young man walked into the masjid of the Prophet ﷺ and asked permission to commit *zinā* (adultery), the Prophet ﷺ spoke to him patiently and kindly.⁴² He could have easily reminded him about the jurisprudential rulings about adultery, and the prescribed punishment - no doubt, that would be unapologetically speaking the truth. But it would not have achieved the intended outcome, so the Prophet ﷺ had to take the approach that would produce the desired result for the betterment of the young man.

What about all the times in the life of the Prophet ﷺ when harshness was used? Didn't he speak the truth clearly? Yes. There are always going to be situations where this is called for strategically as a tool intended for a specific result. The problem we see online is not of speaking the truth clearly, but one of expressing it in a harsh way such that people are turned off. And worse, people who respond to the harshness with cheerleading and zealousness instead of genuine care and concern for the one who is wrong to gain some sense of rectification.

Social media, as a tool, serves to provide validation for the one commenting more than anything else. This is why discussions devolve into debates instead of productive discussion. Aside from the more obvious negative consequences, there is a spiritual cost as well. Imam Malik said, "Quarreling and disputing with regard to knowledge causes the light of knowledge to go away."⁴³

Short-term focus causes people to worry about saving face, or what their reputation will be with their followers. Debates

---

42 Musnad Ahmad
43 *Siyar A'lam al-Nubala'*

sometimes continue endlessly until people forget what they were trying to prove in the first place.

The Prophet ﷺ said, "I guarantee a house in Paradise for one who gives up arguing, even if he is correct. I guarantee a house in the middle of Paradise for one who abandons lying even while joking. I guarantee a house in the highest part of Paradise for one who has good manners."[44]

Winning an argument online is like when people say, "the operation was a success, but the patient died." New controversies pop up on a daily basis online, particularly in Muslim social media circles. Sometimes they relate to classical scholarly debates that have not been settled for over 1,000 years, and sometimes they are about issues like modern social or political topics. These controversies flood our feeds and group chats.

Underneath all of this is a sincere intention. *Dawah*.

There is a drive to spread the truth, correct misinformation, and prevent people from being misled. They produce a short-term coupled with a long-term loss. Second-order effects are the consequences of the consequences of your actions. If you eat a big bowl of ice cream, the first-order effect is enjoyment and a full stomach. The second-order effect is weight gain or bad health. Second-order effects are often the opposite of first-order effects.

True success comes when the second-order effects are positive. That means the immediate consequences of an action may not be entirely positive. We understand this approach when it

---

44 Abu Dawūd

comes to things like education. Study hard now, so you can establish a good career later.

What about *dawah*? The first-order effects of *dawah* come mostly in the form of social media validation such as likes, retweets, shares, comments, notoriety, and platform. Platform is the key one here because it is the one that has the facade of benefit. The more people I can reach, the more *dawah* I can make. Follower counts translate into credibility, and from this comes invites, honorariums, and online courses. The increase in platform is a first-order effect. When someone is focused on it, they are incentivized to accumulate more "wins" to increase this platform. And in the social media age, the old adage of "if it bleeds, it leads" has never been truer.

The most efficient way to increase your platform (and thus, the ability to do *dawah* in a person's mind) is to do things that get attention. This comes by way of refutations, debates, hot takes, personal attacks, tabloid-style personal discussions, and saying things purely for shock value. One second-order effect of this type of *dawah* is that it burns people out. I remember seeing people in the early 2000s engaging in exactly this same type of culture - refutations, debates, and airing of scholarly issues in public forums. Many of these people lost their drive for learning and *dawah* work. In some cases, sadly, they stopped regularly practicing the religion altogether.

Another second-order effect is that it will undermine a person's credibility. Remember that first and second-order consequences are often opposites. A person can build credibility and a platform in the short-term with the very same type of *dawah* that will undermine it in the long-term. As people mature in their understanding of religion, they will realize what type of knowledge truly benefits. And they will see that those caught up in the "issue of the day" were not providing knowledge that truly benefits a person in their relationship with Allah. That will cause them to look at these Islamic personalities with a deep sense of regret, and even anger at having wasted time consuming so much of their content. In extreme cases, this type of *dawah* will be looked back as being performative - increasing a person's social capital as opposed to actually furthering a cause. Much of the discourse around arguing various types of "isms" falls into this category. This breeds a deep level of resentment.

What does *dawah* look like when it is focused on second-order effects instead? It's the slow brick-by-brick building of communities that does not appear to have an immediate payoff. It's spending time in a classroom teaching for years and cultivating students. It looks like effective khutbahs that bring incremental change on a weekly basis compounding into bigger results years down the road. It is the drip by drip effect of giving a *khatirah* (short reminder) after *'isha* to your community every night knowing that it may take years to see the effect. It means investing in people - sacrificing your own time and effort - in order to help and serve.

Long-term *dawah* means doing the unglamorous things you're supposed to do - visiting someone when they are sick, comforting a family on the loss of a loved one, and dropping off a meal when you know someone is having a tough day.

These are the things that will not get immediate gratification in the form of follower counts and other vanity metrics that short-term focus causes us to become infatuated with. Perhaps most difficult, it means eschewing the Muslim social media scene in favor of reading a book or spending time in contemplation to better formulate and refine thoughts before they are presented in public. The first-order effect is that this will not increase your platform, or even get you any type of immediate reward.

The second-order effect, however, is that you may actually fulfill the purpose of meaningfully making *dawah*, adding true value to the lives of others, and being a light by which others come closer to Allah.

The responsibility of this falls not only on the one making *dawah*, but those of us on the other side as well. We will not change this until we better incentivize and reward the right type of *dawah*. Stop liking, sharing, and commenting on the things that only impact the short-term. Seek out and amplify the *dawah* and education that is beneficial for the long-term.

ACTION ITEMS

1) When you find yourself engaging in a debate online, hit the pause button. Assess why you are getting involved, and what type of outcome you hope to achieve

2) What is your ratio of online to offline *dawah*? How many offline conversations do you engage in? What is your level of effort in volunteering for your local community?

3) If you have broken off a relationship with someone because of an online argument, reach out and attempt to sincerely reconcile.

CHAPTER TWELVE

#2Faces

The Prophet ﷺ said, "*Verily, among the worst of people is one with two faces, he who comes with one face to these and another to those.*"[45]

Social media is the ultimate trap of creative avoidance. We'd rather talk about what we're going to do rather than doing it. We fill our time with things we think are important, but in the long run really don't matter.

It is like saying you are starting a business. You go online and let everyone know you are starting one. You post on social media about it, you share inspirational entrepreneurship quotes, you get a logo developed, make business cards, set up a website, set up new social media accounts using your business name, post more stuff on those social accounts - all the while not yet actually having a single paying client.

The influencer culture is notorious for this. People will rent exotic cars, or stage photoshoots at studios made to mimic be-

---

[45] Bukhārī and Muslim

ing on a private jet with the intent of selling and profiting off the image of a particular lifestyle.

Imagine if someone said their dream was to become a doctor and then they ordered a stethoscope online, posted pictures of themselves wearing it, started telling people about which med schools they were looking at, joined online groups for aspiring medical students to get their advice, had their parents tell all potential spouses they were going to be a doctor - but then never actually took the MCAT and applied to medical school?

Once we post something, it feels like we already acted the part. The more we talk about something, or think about doing it, the more we deplete ourselves cognitively and think we're actually accomplishing something.

The examples above may seem extreme, but they are analogous to all types of behavior that we see. Parents may post online about all these amazing things they do with their kids, while the kids feel the parents are actually absent from their lives. We see people who post about how amazing they are doing at work, when in reality they may be on the brink of being let go.

> "Blank spaces, begging to be filled in with thoughts, with photos, with stories. With what we're going to do, with what things should or could be like … Almost universally, the kind of performance we give on social media is positive. It's more 'Let me tell you how well things are going. Look how great I am.' It's rarely the truth: 'I'm scared. I'm struggling. I don't know.'"[46]

---

46 Ryan Holiday, *Ego is the Enemy*

The ability to post only particular types of content lets us shape an online persona that may be drastically different from how we operate in real life. It is easy for someone to post religious sayings and build a following as some type of Islamic scholar or thought leader even though they may have never even delivered a single khutbah in their local community.

Social media has empowered people to not only misrepresent themselves but take on false and anonymous identities altogether. It is not uncommon to see Islamic discussions full of comments from people with pseudonyms that cannot be traced back to a real person.

In Islamic sciences, when a narrator of hadith was *majhool* (unknown), it generally meant their narrations would be rejected. In the online world, fake personalities can quickly garner large followings and become authoritative figures.

People use fake personas to troll friends, or stalk others such as an ex-spouse or potential spouse. Needless to say, this type of behavior is extremely unethical and should be avoided.

The ultimate question here - as always - boils down to intention. Why do you want to be portrayed a certain way? Who are you hoping to show this version of yourself to? What do you get from doing this?

A good rule of thumb learned from our pious predecessors when it comes to portraying a certain image: work to hide your good deeds even more than you hide your bad ones.

ACTION ITEMS

1) Delete fake profiles that you are using, especially if it is being used for a less than pure objective.

2) Share highlights of your life with a smaller circle of family and friends instead of posting on social media.

3) When going through your social feeds, view everything with a personal filter. Realize that no one has a perfect life, and no one has a life as good as what they portray online. Be regular in making *duā* for Allah to continue to bless the good people have, and to make you better than the image you portray online.

CHAPTER THIRTEEN

#Spirituality

Islam online is a relatively new phenomenon. The late 90s and early 00s laid the groundwork for the rapid acceleration of online Islamic activity. Websites became easier to make, so organizations started creating an online presence. Books were converted to PDF format for rapid spread. Message boards and online chat rooms enabled collaboration and interaction for all different types of Muslims all over the world. Even peer-to-peer platforms normally used for illegally pirating music were used to spread recitations of Qur'an and recordings of lectures by Islamic personalities.

This manner of introducing people to Islamic knowledge was a drastic departure from the traditional methods. It broke the confines of learning only through a teacher, or through regular community interactions. Even those who may have previously been criticized for self-study relied heavily on books and other such material. For the first time, people were introduced to unfiltered material, on every subject, with the ability to discuss those with anyone around the world instantly.

People who did not know the fundamentals of the religion were suddenly debating and worrying about esoteric minutiae. Depending on the particular online communities a person was part of, different issues would be en vogue at different times. Spirited debates over whether things like the use of prayer beads or lines in the masjid carpet were abhorrent innovations or not dominated online and then offline discourse.

When people from across the globe were hanging out on a message board actively commenting on an issue, it seemed like the most important thing in the world at that moment in time. This was compounded by the fact that you would log into a messenger app and be bombarded with messages asking if you had seen the latest. Looking back now, it seems like an almost tabloid way to learn the religion - reacting to relatively inconsequential issues instead of building a foundation.

The level of engagement in religious discourse gave off the impression of a proportional level of religiosity. The unfortunate reality is that there was a huge spiritual void, and it simply could not be filled by focusing on the revolving issues of the day. But because everyone was so caught up in making their views known, tearing apart someone else's views, and winning imaginary internet points over these arguments, the lack of spirituality became the proverbial elephant in the room.

In the years since, many platforms have disappeared or been replaced. It is likely that in a few years, the ones we use now will also be replaced by other tools and platforms. What remains the same is the hyperconnectivity, and the ability of these platforms to focus our attention into reactive issues. It is important to understand the impact of digital media on our communities and individual spirituality.

Online communities can serve to complement, compete with, or replace our physical communities.

Most of our local masjids were initially established with a limited scope. Families got together to create spaces to hold Sunday school and Friday prayers. As these communities grew, Imams and scholars were brought in for guidance. The local masjid became an institution for community building and the primary source of spiritual nourishment. Families befriended each other out of shared religious identity, physical proximity, and common values and goals.

It was not uncommon for a child to be born into a community, and have the same Imam perform his or her *ʿaqīqah* and also *nikkah*. There was a sense of trust and stability with the local religious leadership. They were entrusted with the spiritual development and pastoral care of the community. The topics discussed from the pulpit, the content of classes, and the personal care provided all emanated from a qualified source accountable to the community.

This, of course, had its own set of issues. What if the community leadership is toxic? What if your community is not able to attract qualified religious figures?

While these issues have persisted, the advent of the smartphone completely disrupted both the meaning of local community, and our relationship to it.

Our religious experiences are no longer connected to the physical community. We can connect ourselves to seemingly any community in the world. If the local masjid is not catering to our needs, we can find viable alternatives online.

At a deeper level, technology empowered people to be active participants and have their voices heard. Prior to this, if there was friction in the local masjid, you had to tough it out and fight it. In some ways, working through issues strengthened community ties. Now, however, we have options - and new expectations.

If we are free to participate in online communities, why does the local community shut us out?

I am free to pursue education, activism, or other projects with people I'm digitally connected to. Why am I not able to do the same in the local masjid?

I'm connected now to new causes and issues affecting Muslims around the globe. Why is my local Muslim community oblivious to them?

It can be frustrating to see movement and action online, and come to the local masjid and feel an overwhelming sense of inertia. Our local leaders may not be in tune with the same issues we are encountering and investing time in.

The online world is focused on the individual. We go online to find what we can learn about our religion that is relevant to our personal situations. We seek out ways to advocate for causes we care about. We seek to connect with people who are similar to us. In other words, it is conducive to personalization.

Local communities, however, are not. They must serve the spiritual needs of an entire congregation. This means that not every community initiative will be aligned to the goals of each individual. A single person in their early 20's, for example, may not see the need to dedicate their own time, energy, or money to the building of a school for young children.

These types of conflicts have always existed, but the internet has exacerbated those divides. We are no longer forced to maintain a commitment to our local community as we were before. Instead, we are able to seek out our own individual purpose to pursue.

The internet took control away from the local masjid. The community or Imam lost its place as the reference point or authority.

For the masjid, this raises new questions. Remaining relevant requires a new type of intentionality regarding its purpose. How can the masjid create a community in which diverse points of view are expressed without fear of reprisal? What work is the masjid doing to improve society, the community, and the individual lives of congregation members? How does the masjid foster the building of relationships? How does the masjid balance the needs of the local community while still being connected to national and global causes? How can individual congregation members be empowered to contribute meaningfully?

The incentive to fight for and change the local community is disappearing quickly. The path of least resistance is finding ways to learn and contribute online.

This raises a question though, how healthy is it to seek spirituality online?

Social media platforms make access to learning significantly easier. We can connect with people who raise our īmān, read high quality written articles, take detailed classes, and attend virtual events.

For those without a strong local community, this is a lifesaver. It does, however, require caution.

In an average day, a person may consume dozens of Islamic nuggets or tidbits – short reminders on a wide array of religious topics. After a whole day of reading, liking, and re-sharing these reminders, a person can feel accomplished. It gives off the illusion of having learned a lot due to the frequency of exposure and breadth of topics. It is important not to let these types of reminders inadvertently displace the process of deeper learning.

On the other end of the spectrum, online echo chambers may convince someone to go deep into a rabbit hole that ultimately brings no benefit. Imagine a person who does not know Arabic and has not formally studied any sciences of *tafsīr* staying up all night studying the intricacies of Qur'anic abrogation, only to miss *fajr* prayer.

The biggest loss resulting from the disconnect of our personal relationship with the local community is the loss of grounding and the loss of a sense of prioritization.

Our approach should be to take full advantage of the resources we have online while simultaneously pushing ourselves to build stronger in-person community ties. This requires both an individual effort, and an institutional one.

Personal spiritual development is in need of a strong communal element. We need to find ways to cultivate deeper bonds of brotherhood and sisterhood with those in our communities.

In the same way that the masjid must reckon with its purpose, we as congregants have our own challenges. What can we do to help build community with those closest to us?

ACTION ITEMS

1) Start attending a local masjid weekly class or monthly program if you are not already doing that.

2) Find ways to organize regular meetups with people in your area. This can be anything from a family picnic, a potluck group, or a book club.

3) If you are benefitting from an online Islamic program, look for ways to include others. Watch those programs together with friends or family and discuss your reflections.

CHAPTER FOURTEEN

#OPTIMISM

When Ibrahim (as) famously left Hājar (as) with their baby son in the desert, she asked him if Allah commanded him to leave them. He said yes, so she said that she trusted Allah would take care of them. Her response to the situation illuminated a middle path between two extremes we commonly see.

One extreme is pessimism. A person may simply give up and lose hope. After scanning the horizon and seeing no food, water, or any sign of civilization, it would be easy to sit down and do nothing. People with a negative mindset will focus on all the things wrong in this situation - "there's no food, we'll probably die here" - and overwhelm themselves with hopelessness.

The other extreme is naive optimism. It is sitting there doing nothing while telling yourself everything will work out. Or perhaps to simply "envision" a better situation and hope it will arrive.

Hājar demonstrated what optimism looks like.

The action of her heart was to trust Allah and have faith that He would make a way out. The action of her limbs was to do everything in her control to remedy the situation. No food? Then she will run back and forth between mountains looking for something to give her child.

She set a precedent that embodies the prophetic tradition, "Tie your camel, and then trust in Allah."[47]

When it comes to the sunnah of the Prophet ﷺ we rarely talk about *mindsets*. The sunnah of optimism provides a playbook for dealing with the major and minor difficulties in our lives.

It's amazing to think that he was tested more than anyone else, and yet, his default demeanor was always smiling.

True optimism provides the resolve to deal with difficulty.

When we look back at the most difficult moments of our lives, we actually cherish them. Those hardships, failures, and scars are what made us into who we are today. They made us stronger and provided lessons so invaluable we'd never trade them for anything.

This is easy in hindsight, but harder to do in the moment - "Patience is at the first strike of calamity."[48]

The prophetic example shows us how to cultivate a mindset of optimism.

The Prophet ﷺ warned against giving up on people. "Whoever says the people are destroyed, he is the most destroyed amongst them."[49] And Allah says in the Qur'an, "Do not lose

---

47 Tirmīdhī
48 Bukhārī and Muslim
49 Muslim

heart or despair, and you will be superior if you are [true] believers."⁵⁰

Despair is easy to feel almost by default. Every time we turn on our phones we are bombarded with headlines, photos, and videos of injustices that make it seem as if the world is full of hopelessness. It is difficult to feel anything but despair when we see increasingly toxic and polarizing discourse around every issue of religious or social significance. It can feel like things are spiraling out of control with no way to rein them in.

The lens of the believer necessitates understanding that our faith in Allah means knowing Allah is the source of all that is good, and He will never decree something in which the evil outweighs the good - even if that good is reserved for the ākhirah.

The Prophet ﷺ, even in the most dire circumstances, would look for excuses to be optimistic. When the Muslims set out for *umrah*, and were blocked by the Quraysh, the situation was tense. Negotiators kept coming but no agreement could be reached. Finally, the Quraysh sent Suhayl b. Amr, and the Prophet ﷺ took this as a good sign. The name Suhayl gives the meaning of "easy", and so the Prophet ﷺ announced to his companions that this was a sign their affairs would be easy. Eventually, the treaty of Hudaybiyah was agreed upon - a victory in and of itself, even if it was unclear at the time as to how.

He even engineered the environment around him to be one that instills optimism. When he met someone from a place called the "Valley of Misguidance", he renamed it the "Valley of

---

50 3:139

Guidance". This shows us that the way we refer to things even has a subconscious effect on us. What is the subconscious effect, for example, of referring to one's spouse as "the old ball and chain" over and over again? When his grandson was born, Alī named him *Ḥarb* (war). The Prophet ﷺ changed his name to Hasan (good).[51]

When it comes to social media, we can follow this example in culling our online environment. Do we follow accounts that instill within us a sense of optimism, or despair? What image do we portray of ourselves? What types of comments do we leave when discussing community, social, political, or religious issues? What type of screen name or usernames do we give ourselves? All of these contribute to creating an optimistic environment.

He encouraged his companions to always be of those spreading good to others. He instructed them, "Give glad tidings, and do not scare people away. Make things easy, do not make things difficult."[52]

The very nature of social media is reason enough to be optimistic about it. When social networking sites first spread, we did not know how to use them. We posted mundane updates throughout our day. It took quite a bit of trial and error to figure out that these platforms could be used to do things like staying in touch with family more regularly. It took some evolution before we started using these platforms to teach religion or dis-

---

51 Al-Bukhārī, *al-Adab al-Mufrad*.
52 Bukhārī

cuss politics. And as maddening as the discourse around them may be, we have every reason to believe these platforms will continue to evolve and change.

ACTION ITEMS

1) Monitor the comments you leave on the posts of friends, or even when messaging a corporation online. How often do you post comments with negative emotions compared to positive ones?

2) Send a message of encouragement or appreciation to a friend. We are quick to correct or point out mistakes, but much slower at identifying and calling out positive behaviors.

3) Look for opportunities to share positive or uplifting stories to your friends circle or social media channels - especially during times where people feel an overwhelm of negativity.

CHAPTER FIFTEEN

#ActionPlan

Given all these negative effects, should we not just abandon all these services?

Ideally, yes. The overwhelmingly negative effects of social media are well-documented. Regardless, we find ourselves coming back due to the lack of alternatives. Until we find another way to replace the feeling of connection that social media provides, it will be difficult to convince people to quit completely – no matter how beneficial it may be.

The following five steps provide a framework to guide our usage of social media.

1. Intention

There are a number of tough questions: Why do you choose to follow, friend, unfollow, or unfriend someone? Why do you utilize social media? Why are you posting or sharing a particular status update? Who are you targeting when you write something? What kind of response are you seeking? What about sharing something you may not have read just to look intelligent or give off the persona of a social activist?

What about liking or commenting on someone's status? Did you like it or share because it provided value? Or maybe to try and get the attention of the person posting?

Intention is at the core of any action. It is famously said the intention should be checked before a deed, while performing a deed, and after the deed is done.

Some people use social media for entertainment. Some see it as a productivity tool, or even a business need. Others see it as a way to be politically or socially active. Some use it to simply stay in touch with family and friends. Many use it as a combination of all of these.

One of the most fascinating things about social media is that it sometimes uncovers our true intentions. It gives us an outlet to carefully craft a certain persona. We share things that cause us to be perceived a certain way. We carefully write out our biographies, highlight certain quotes, and find the perfect profile picture to make a statement about who we think we truly are. Sometimes we do not even realize the true intention behind what we are trying to convey.

Assess your intention before posting, while sharing, and after checking the likes and comments to try and maintain sincerity. Doing this requires a high level of self-awareness. You must be able to critically assess why you interact the way that you do.

The more challenging part is slowing down enough to check your intention in the fast-paced, first-draft, shoot-from-the-hip culture of the internet.

The payoff to slowing down, though, is immeasurable.

Ultimately, whatever your intention for posting, following,

liking, sharing, or consuming is, you must be comfortable with that intention as it relates to your accountability with Allah.

The easiest way to do this is always keeping this Prophetic advice front and center – "He who believes in Allah and the Last Day must either speak good or remain silent."[53]

2. Unplug

When we exercise physically, we take rest days. When we have a busy day at work, we take a mental break. We take block out time each year to take vacations.

Unplugging does not mean we deactivate all our accounts and downgrade our phones. It does mean we need to build in the digital equivalent of rest time and vacation days. What that looks like depends on how drastically you want to cut your usage. My recommendation would be to start small, and keep experimenting with the suggested solutions below.

Notifications

Take time to go through your settings and turn off as many notifications as you possibly can. Disable the red badges, disable the push notifications, and disable any buzzes or sounds. Do this for social media apps, emails, group chats, and anything else that tries to get your attention.

When left unregulated, these apps will fill up all your free time, and demand your attention even when you are doing something else.

---

53 Muslim

Disabling notifications better empowers you to deal with those platforms on your own terms. This may not significantly reduce the total volume of time spent on social media, but it cuts down on the short, repetitive, and disruptive checking of the phone.

Downtimes

We all need protected time during the day. Without intentionally blocking it, our phones will fill it by default. While some people have the ability to stick to a strict schedule of limiting their screen time to a fixed amount, this is not a viable or sustainable solution for most.

Find pockets of time to designate as off-limits. Half an hour before bedtime, and half an hour after waking up are ideal. Making family breakfast or dinner time screen-free goes a long way in cultivating quality time. Other things to make off-limits would be while driving, during work meetings, or while in class.

Setting time limits on usage helps to facilitate more downtime as well. There are always options for configuring screen time usage, or having social media apps alert you after a certain period of time that you have hit a preset limit. These tools are not foolproof, but provide a guide to help mitigate against overuse.

Uninstall

Many people attempt to deactivate accounts, only to reactivate after a period of days, weeks, and sometimes even months.

A more sustainable option would be to uninstall social media applications from your phone (that is always with you), and restrict your usage of those apps on other devices. This cuts down significantly on repetitive usage while still leaving you feeling assured of not missing out on anything important.

3. Unfollow

The people we interact with most are the ones we follow online. Some of them are not even people, they are often organizations or companies. Throughout the day we check our feeds and messages on multiple apps.

If I see short status updates from a celebrity 15 times a day, every day, then that is the person I am keeping company with. That is more often than I interact with people I would consider to be close friends.

What type of messaging are you consuming every time you turn on your computer or take your phone out of your pocket? Your feed should be highly curated to bring benefit to your life and your ākhirah.

Unfollow relentlessly.

Unfollow anyone who shares updates that are toxic, that bring negativity, or are even just annoying. Your feed is a place to exercise being selfish. If an account does not positively contribute to your life, then unfollow.

This goes for unfollowing discussions in addition to people. It can be tempting to go down various rabbit holes while following trending discussions, or even the news. Exercise that same level of restraint. If a discussion is not of direct benefit for you, remove yourself from it.

4. Prioritize

What is the best use of your time at any given moment?

Family dinner time may not be the best time to use your phone. The same goes for driving, or during a work meeting (especially if you are being paid to attend that meeting). These are obvious times to not use your phone or check social media.

On the other hand, waiting in line at the grocery store does not present any real competing priorities. Catching up on social media at times like this would be relatively harmless.

I had a conversation with my barber once who mentioned that his wife ran her wedding planning business primarily from her phone. This made it difficult to enjoy dinner, or watch a movie, because her attention was always drawn to running the business. He said it annoyed him, but he also did not complain because that business was a priority in terms of maintaining their household.

There will always be situations like this where priorities can compete and there is not a clear-cut way out. It is important to identify your priorities for yourself, and your family, and then find ways to stick to them.

5. Supplement

It is almost a laughable cliché (unfortunately) to tell people to imagine if they spent as much time reading Qur'an as they do on social media. The default function of these devices is to occupy our time. Downtime will happen only with intentionality.

The more you find yourself interacting with people online, the more important it is to schedule time for in-person meetups.

The more you consume information online (Islamic or otherwise), the more important it becomes to attend classes in person, have group discussions, or simply read physical books.

In short, your online time needs a constant complement of active offline time.

Conclusion

It is famously said that the only constant is change. Our methods of communicating and interacting have changed considerably in a short span of time. It is only expected that they will continue to change. New forms of media will be developed. New technologies will be invented.

No matter how much things change, our religious principles are timeless. The guidance we find in the Qur'an and in the *Sunnah* of our beloved Prophet ﷺ are perfect until the end of time.

The challenge, as always, is in the implementation. We must always strive to connect the dots of what we know from our faith and apply it to our daily lives. This is what will equip us to lead a change and model a higher standard of behavior in utilizing and engaging with social media.

This book is a small effort in service of that goal, and I pray that Allah accepts it.

Acknowledgements

The Prophet ﷺ said, "Whoever is not grateful to people is not grateful to Allah."[54]

I have to start by first thanking my parents. There is no possible way to list all the ways they have supported me, instilled confidence in me, and encouraged me. I am forever indebted to them.

My wife, Fousia, who not only pushed me to do this book, but who has supported me throughout this process and sacrificed many weekends so I could teach, and many evenings so I could write.

My kids, because they said there is no way I can write a book without mentioning their names in it. Thank you AbdurRaheem, Aisha, Haniyah, and Musa.

My sister Zainah for not only her general help and support, but for the selfless effort in editing and making my writing sound better than it is.

Shaykh AbdulNasir, my long-time close friend and mentor – this project simply does not exist without him. Thank you for

---

54 Tirmīdhī

ACKNOWLEDGEMENTS

believing in this project and providing a platform for it. Your counsel, advice, and support, and everything else have been invaluable.

I must thank many of the Imams and Shuyukh who have helped along the way. Shaykh Nomaan Baig was the first person to invite me to present on this topic and started the chain reaction that led to this book. Shaykh Yaser Birjas, Mufti Hussain Kamani, Imam Omar Suleiman, Shaykh Mohammad ElShinawy, Shaykh Mohamed Hussein, Shaykh Mikaeel Smith, Mufti Muntasir Zaman, Shaykh Navaid Aziz, Shaykh Hasib Noor, Shaykh Ammar alShukry, and many others – all of you have contributed to this.

Shaykh Salmaan Nasir, my lifelong friend since birth, for not only reviewing the content but answering my nonstop questions throughout.

Thank you to my friends who pushed me to write this book and have provided feedback throughout the process, Imran Haq, Mohammed Faris, Adam Taufique, Waleed Jameel, and Naufil Mulla.

Thank you Amnah Sultan for the wonderful cover design.

And thank you to all those who contributed to this work in some way who I may have neglected to mention.

If there is one thing I learned in the process of writing this book, it is that it is impossible without the sacrifice of others. I pray that Allah blesses you and your families with the best of this life and the next, and that whatever good comes of this book is a *ṣadaqah jāriyah* for you all.

ALSO BY THE AUTHOR

To follow my writing and
join the email newsletter, please visit
http://ibnabeeomar.com

Podcast on faith-based personal
development is hosted at
http://ibnabeeomar.simplecast.com

YouTube channel focused on
book reviews can be found at
http://youtube.com/c/OmarUsman

If you would like to pass along any comments,
questions, or feedback, please email
omarusman@ibnabeeomar.com

www.ingramcontent.com/pod-product-compliance
Lightning Source LLC
Chambersburg PA
CBHW070434010526
44118CB00014B/2035